Mom and I

by Hareem Atif Khan • illustrated by Lisa Hunt

Lucy Calkins and Michael Rae-Grant, Series Editors

LETTER-SOUND CORRESPONDENCES

m, t, a, n, s, ss, p, i,
d, g, o, c, k, ck, r, u,
h, b, e, f, ff, l, ll, z,
j, w, y, x, -e, -o, -y,
ch, sh, **th**

HIGH-FREQUENCY WORDS

is, like, see, the, as, has, too, of, says, to, for, look, you, do

Mom and I
Author: Hareem Atif Khan
Series Editors: Lucy Calkins and Michael Rae-Grant

Heinemann
145 Maplewood Avenue, Suite 300
Portsmouth, NH 03801
www.heinemann.com

Cataloging-in-Publication data is on file with the Library of Congress.

ISBN-13: 978-0-325-13844-2

Design and Production: Dinardo Design LLC, Carole Berg, and Rebecca Anderson

Editors: Anna Cockerille and Jennifer McKenna

Illustrations: Lisa Hunt

Photographs: p. 32 (top left) © Pavel Adashkevich/Shutterstock; p. 32 (top right, bottom right) © fizkes/Shutterstock; p. 32 (bottom left) © yurakrasil/Shutterstock; inside back cover (left) © Brocreative/Shutterstock; inside back cover (right) © Caleb Foster/Shutterstock.

Manufacturing: Gerard Clancy

Printed in Dongguan, China
4 5 6 7 8 9 10 TP 28 27 26 25 24 23
April 2023 Printing / PO# 4500868396

Contents

Meet...

Imran   Mom   Yasmin

The Job List

I run up and hug Mom.

"Let's go!" she says.

We stop at the red hand
that tells you not to cross.
A big bus zips by.

Mom has a list of jobs for us.

"Can we get a snack too?" I ask.

"You bet," she says.

I check the list.

"The next job is to get

the wash," I tell Mom.

We go up the block.
Then, we bump into
my pal, Yasmin.

The dryer spins and spins.

The moms chat and chat.

I check the list.

"The next job is to get milk,"
I tell Mom.

As we go up the block,

we do this and that.

Bump,

bump,

bump!

Then, we go up the steps.

Up and up and up...

"This last job is NOT fun,"

I tell Mom.

On the top step, we see a box.

"Is that for us?" I ask.

Yoga Mat

I rip the top off the box.

"Um...this is just a mat."

"This is not just a mat,"
Mom says. "It is a yoga mat."

I criss-cross my legs
and sit next to Mom
on the yoga mat.

16

OK!

17

20

I try it, but my legs flop,

and I land on my back.

"Not bad, Imran!" says Mom.

I Can Do Yoga!

"I can't do yoga," I tell Mom.

"Not like you can."

"You can if you try," says Mom.
"Let's do Up Dog."

Mom has me lift my chest
and my chin up.
"This is Up Dog," she says.
"See? You can do it!"

"This is fun!" I tell Mom.
"But I still can't do that
hand stand."

"Well," says Mom.

"Let's try it step by step."

Mom helps me bend.

"This is step 1," she says.

Next, Mom tells me to kick up.
"This is step 2," she says.

Mom helps me lift my legs.

"This is step 3," she says.

"Try not to slip!"

"Mom!" I yell.

"Look! I can do the hand stand!
I can do yoga!"

YOGA

Yoga is a kind of exercise that calms your body and calms your mind. People do yoga for lots of reasons: to be healthy, to relax, and to build up their muscles nice and strong.

monkey

crow

Yoga is one of the oldest kinds of exercise in the world. It was invented more than 5,000 years ago in India, but

om

scorpion

these days people all over the world do yoga. To do yoga, you need a mat. Roll your mat out on the floor and try some *asanas,* or yoga poses.

If you keep practicing yoga, you will grow strong and flexible. *Flexible* means you can flex, or bend, your body in lots of ways. If you grow *really* strong and flexible, then you might try some of these expert yoga poses!

Talk about...

Ask your reader some questions like...

- What happened in this book?

- Turn to page 23. How was Imran feeling in this part? Why was that? (If the student says *mad* or *sad,* acknowledge they're correct, then supply the more specific word *frustrated.*)

- In this book, Mom picks up Imran from school. How is it the same or different from the way you get picked up from school?